*In Our Own Words*

# *In Our Own Words*

Stories by Australia's international students

Edited by Donna Lee Brien, Alison Owens and
Janene Carey

Tablelands Press
Armidale, NSW

Tablelands Press

5 Highlands Rd Armidale NSW 2350

National Library of Australia Cataloguing-in-Publication data:
Title: In our own words : stories by Australia's international students /
editors: Donna Lee Brien, Alison Owens, Janene Carey.
ISBN 978-0-9924236-3-6 (paperback)
ISBN 978-0-9924236-4-3 (ebook : Kindle)
ISBN 978-0-9924236-5-0 (ebook : epub)
Subjects: Students, Foreign–Australia–Anecdotes. Creative writing.
Australia–Social life and customs–21st century.
Dewey Number: 378.016
This book was created using PressBooks.com with PDF rendering by
Prince XML. Cover credit http://www.selfpubbookcovers.com/BeeJavier

This publication was produced with the
generous sponsorship of a Scholarship of
Learning and Teaching Grant from Central
Queensland University. Human ethics
approval project number H12/04-053.

# Contents

# *Preface*

This book is one of the outcomes from a recent learning and teaching research grant at CQUniversity. The premise of the research study was that, through reflection on their experiences, international students in Australia could become actively involved in the creative production of narratives that enable the richness of their non-standard English to be celebrated. It goes beyond the routine approach of regarding international students as learners of English as an additional language who need simply to become competent in their use of standard English, to one where they are encouraged to 'find their voice' and to 'write their story'. As you will see from the narratives provided within this book, those stories are compelling, describing their experiences of learning about living and learning in Australia in their own words, focusing on creative expression rather than the minutiae of grammar and the 'deficit model' of English usage.

From a learning perspective, humans make greatest gains when they are involved in activities that they are fully engaged with and enjoy, leading to a strong, positive approach to the activities and their outcomes. This is a key feature in Mihaly Csikszantmahalyi's concept of 'flow', where learning is not seen as an imposed requirement, but is embedded in the activity itself. The stories in this book are the result of a process of encouraging international students to take the lead and to flourish as creative writers, with support provided through a series of workshops and collaborations with academic staff. The results speak for themselves, in terms of the students' creative use of language and storytelling.

CQUniversity has a strong tradition of supporting international students in Australia, since they represent more than one-in-four of our higher education students. This book reflects the commitment of the staff involved to supporting innovative and effective approaches to the development of international students as individuals who bring a wealth of experiences to their writing.

But enough from me – far better to spend your time reading the students' own words!

Professor Rob Reed
Pro Vice-Chancellor (Learning and Teaching),
CQUniversity

# Introduction

"Sorry of my English," begins Xiaolu Guo's novel, *A Concise English-Chinese Dictionary for Lovers* and so, in a similar vein, end countless submissions written by over 228,000 international students studying at Australian universities. While readers and critics embraced the narrator's less than perfect English in this novel, and the book was shortlisted for the 2007 Orange Prize for Fiction, many other writers whose first language is not English attract criticism for their efforts to communicate. The tendency to focus on the limitations of international students as rote- and passive-learners who are linguistically unprepared for their study has been termed the 'deficit model' and has persisted for several decades in the Australian higher education sector. This modeling has endured despite a competing 'inclusionary' model, in which such students are recognised and valued as bilingual or multi-lingual learners using English to further their discipline-based knowledge and employment potential in a globalised workforce.

Recent UNESCO figures estimate that over 3.6 million students are studying for a university degree outside of their home country, and many of them are studying in the language medium of English. This compounds the dominance of English as a global language and also as a Lingua Franca by which speakers of diverse first language backgrounds can communicate. Over twenty per cent of students at Australian universities are international learners and the majority are studying in English as their second or third language. There are also increasing numbers of teaching and support staff whose first language is not English. This means that universities are now linguistically complex arenas and, as a result, the textual performances of learners can be complex, and even controversial, in terms of the expectations of academic staff as well as the employers of these graduates once they complete their studies.

However, as the notions of 'Global English' and 'English as a Lingua Franca' become more widely accepted and understood, learners and writers of English as a Second or Additional Language have greater opportunity to construct unique texts in their authentic voice for an increasing, and increasingly interested, English language readership. Alongside this, there is a growing recognition that, while international students tend to be concentrated in certain discipline streams such as management and commerce, there is also interest in creative and other arts areas, including creative writing.

In the context of creative writing, in particular, where textual experimentation is a norm, Learners of English as an Additional Language (LEAL, but frequently still referred to as ESL – English as a Second Language) have the capacity to express important insights and experiences particularly relevant to cultural identity, transformation and understanding. With this as the underpinning rationale, the editors implemented a project that sought to promote the creative writing interests and capacities of a small group of LEAL at an Australian university campus through a personalised workshop and mentoring program. We were influenced by Brian Castro's idea that teaching creative writing in South-East Asia to non-native English speakers does not "mean teaching basic expression, teaching grammar and syntax, teaching rhetoric and composition, although all these things are very important"[1]. Therefore, this project focused on what teaching creative writing does focus on: "a level of imagination far surpassing the ordinary, and a level of intelligent thinking moulded by good reading and an ear for style, tone, language and more language"[1].

Clearly, perceptions about the English skills of LEAL have serious implications for large numbers of students, teachers, employers and, more broadly, the higher education industry in Australia and other dominant English speaking recipient countries including the USA, UK, Canada and New Zealand. Recognising these learners as linguistically complex (rather than deficient) and finding new and enhanced methods to support their language needs, as well as their cultural adjustment, could transform both university practices and the students' experience of those practices. This project suggests that creative writing could be one such approach.

The influence of a specific first language on a second language is manifold, and includes accent, ideographic form, grammatical patterns and other linguistic elements. It is important to recognise that whatever language individuals use, and whatever the individual competence in that language, everyone uses language creatively to describe and engage with the world by constructing and interpreting semantic chunks from the vocabulary and syntax available in their working memory. Language 'immigrants' or 'exophones'[2], however, may use their learned language in a more pragmatically creative sense as a consequence of a smaller bank of vocabulary as well as their personal knowledge of language rules and conventions, often affected by first language characteristics. Says Clifford: "I believe my Russian background adds color and sometimes quirkiness to the way I use English language"[3]. Indeed, in ex-British colonies such as Nigeria, "English has become one of the languages available for use by the creative writer"[4]. Vyleta describes his English as "cobbled together from the many places I have lived and the books I have read, a transnational quilt. It limits me in some respects, and opens avenues in others"[2]. Beauvais feels that, "The mistakes and clumsiness of my English all have a story to tell beyond the story I'm trying to tell"[5].

As McDonald and Busa point out, "People are always saying new things"[6] and, in this way, LEAL are not unique in their creative use of the English language. It is widely accepted that one of the reasons that Shakespeare's writing is so vivid is because of his creation of copious new words and usages. *Referential creativity* is a theoretical approach proposed by McDonald and Busa as useful in understanding how (native) speakers construct new, unusual and, therefore, creative utterances as a result of both their lexical-semantic knowledge and immersion in a specific situation. In such a creative linguistic process, for example, nouns become verbs over time, such as 'ironing', 'faxing' and 'googling', and omissions or substitutions allow utterances that are comprehensible only by referral to the immediate and shared situation of interlocutors, as in 'back up', or 'put out'.

LEAL have both less (English) and more (languages other than English) lexical-syntactic-semantic knowledge than monolingual English speakers. They rely on a more restricted English resource but have alternative language options available to express meaning and that also impact on their English utterances. So, while mother tongue speakers may use their language creatively in response to situational characteristics, LEAL may use English even more creatively as a consequence of situation plus linguistic 'interference'. These utterances are, moreover, completely comprehensible. Examples of LEAL utterances from the authors' teaching experience which appear peculiar (although correct) to a native speaker include: 'tomorrow is newer than today' and 'shallow is when the top of the water is very near the bottom of the water'. These examples also reveal that there is clearly poetic potential in such constructions.

Learning about another culture inevitably involves learning more about your own culture and identity. The transformational capacity of crossing culture and language for extended periods of time is profound, has a significant impact on an individual's approach to learning [7,8] and warrants documentation in the authentic voice of the sojourner. Themes that have emerged to date about international students include the international student as hero [9], victim [10] and 'cash cow'[11,12] but there is still room in this discourse for international students to generate their own metaphors to describe their experiences of studying and living in foreign communities and cultures using their own, unique English voices.

Our project invited a small group of LEAL of any discipline to engage in a series of creative writing activities – a program of workshops and editorial-type mentoring support sessions – during which they would develop, write and edit a piece of creative work reflecting their Australian experience. This guided process focused on generating their sustained authentic-voiced accounts of their cultural and educational sojourn in Australia. From an initial group of seven students, three students (from China and Brazil) completed the project and their stories are published in this booklet. The remaining four students engaged in part of the process but did not persevere with story development to a finished text, perhaps reflecting the heavy cognitive load and stress factors impacting international students.

Although their stories were not intended to represent auto-ethnographically 'true' accounts of their personal experience, they provide compelling reading as both imaginative and auto-biographical narratives. Interestingly, although produced in the context of the university, all stories were set outside of the actual classrooms, buildings and direct communities of that institution. They were, instead, focused on experiences in the wider community, and particularly the world of work. It seemed that in terms of cultural learning, study was a component of their university work, but real learning took place outside the classroom.

The key theme emerging from these narratives is the sheer difficulty of negotiating a new culture and terrain to achieve financial independence and a degree of integration with a community that operates on a different set of rules. Although each narrator experiences some disappointment either in what happens to them or to others, they also positively connect with strangers and take constructive lessons from these experiences, acknowledging their own encultured limitations.

Although we did not specifically direct students to give vent to such experiences, providing an avenue whereby they can be expressed in creative texts provides a range of advantages. It allows readers, such as academic staff as well as other students, to gain better insight into the cross-cultural experience and develop greater empathy for the cultural sojourner. Furthermore, the act of authoring such texts can provide a focused opportunity for LEAL to reflect on, and evaluate, their frustrating or negative experiences and identify gains through transformations. In this sense, the process and the product are empowering both in terms of valuing the LEAL voice and engaging them more intimately, and on a personal level with members of the university and the general community.

All stories are culturally and linguistically reflexive and refer to language and incorporate terms or concepts from other cultures/languages. Creative expressions are plentiful and demonstrate syntactic as well as semantic alternatives to standardised English. In this manner, whilst these texts make sense, they challenge, and perhaps unsettle, the expectations of readers of conventional English. They reveal and enact an approach to English usage that is heavily influenced by other languages, other cultures and by the writers' experiences as learners.

The editorial staff involved in the workshops and in providing ongoing support for these LEAL raised questions with authors about what the meaning of their writing was, if this was obscure, but resisted the reflex to 'correct' expression into a standardised English. The impulse to 'correct' LEAL text was suspended for this program but nevertheless, the impulse is deeply ingrained and the experience provided an opportunity for the researchers to reflect on their own textual response habits in the context of recognising and promoting the legitimacy of LEAL expression.

We found that encouraging and supporting LEAL to write creative texts certainly improved their capacity to express themselves in their learned language. It also not only encouraged their willingness to thus express themselves, but also mobilised a (perhaps previously untapped) interest in creative writing, with all participants expressing interest in further workshops and opportunities to produce creative texts. On our part, as teachers of creative writing, we found that being involved in such an activity went some way to addressing the dominant tendency to critique, correct and reject the voices of LEAL.

We hope that you enjoy the following stories authored by Lili, Elaine and Emily.

Donna Lee Brien<br>Alison Owens<br>Janene Carey

***

For a fuller description of the rationale for the project, the pedagogical processes involved, as well as an analysis of the outcomes for participants and the implications for EAL learners and their teachers, please see:

Owens, A. & Brien, D.L. (2014) Writing themselves: using creative writing to facilitate international student accounts of their intercultural experience. *New Writing: The International Journal for the Practice and Theory of Creative Writing*, Available online at: http://dx.doi.org/10.1080/14790726.2014.932815.

## Notes

1. Castro, B. (2011) Teaching creative writing in Asia: four points and five provocations. *TEXT Special Issue Website Series* 10 (April), edited by Jane Camens and Dominique Wilson, 1–8. Available online at: http://www.textjournal.com.au/speciss/issue10/content.htm.

2. Vyleta, D. (2012) Dan Vyleta's top 10 books in second languages. *The Guardian*, 16 Feb 2011. Available online at: http://www.theguardian.com/books/2011/feb/16/dan-vyleta-top-10-books-second-languages.

3. Clifford, N. (2012) Writing a novel, English as a second language. *Art of Storytelling*. Available online at:

http://artofstorytelling.wordpress.com/2012/07/24/ writing-a-novel-english-as-a-second-language.

4. Bisong, J. (1995) Language choice and cultural imperialism: a Nigerian perspective. *ELT Journal* 49 (2), 122-132.

5. Beauvais, C. (2012) What's the word? – Writing fiction in your second language. Available online at: http://www.clementinebeauvais.com/eng/2012/04/15/ whats-the-word-writing-fiction-in-your-second-language.

6. McDonald, D.D. & Busa, F. (1994) On the creative use of language: the form of lexical resources. *7th International Generation Workshop*, Kennebunkport, Maine June 21-24, 1994, Available online at: http://aclweb.org/anthology/ W/W94/W94-0310.pdf.

7. Brien, D.L. (2007) Developing and enhancing creativity: a case study of the special challenges of teaching writing in Hong Kong. *TEXT: The Journal of the Australian Association of Writing Programs*, 12(1), April. Available online at: http://www.textjournal.com.au.

8. Owens, A. (2011) Supporting and evaluating transitional learning for international university students, *Australian Universities Review*, 53 (1) available online at: http://www.aur.org.au/

9. Hart, W.B. (1999) The intercultural sojourn as the hero's journey, *The Edge: the E-Journal of Intercultural Relations*, 2 (1) (n.p.) HART-LI.COMmunications. Available online at: http://www.hart-li.com/biz/theedge/.

10. Rodan, P. (2009) The international student as student, migrant and victim. *Australian Universities' Review*, 51 (2) 27-31.

11. Narushima, Y. (2008) Overseas students exploited as cash cows. *The Sydney Morning Herald*, December 17, 2008, Available online at: http://www.smh.com.au/news/

national/overseas-students-exploited-as-cash-cows/
2008/12/16/1229189622969.html.

12. Trounson, A. (2011) Universities accused of milking
foreign students. *The Australian*, October 28, 2011.
Available online at: http://www.theaustralian.com.au/
higher-education/universities-accused-of-milking-
foreign-students/story-e6frgcjx-1226178913388.

# My Transformation Process from Chinese to Australian Culture

## By Lili Wu

When I walked inside the airport waiting zone and waved the biggest good bye to my mother on 14th June, 2012, I suddenly felt I had abandoned my whole world. Yet there was neither deep sorrow nor extreme happiness and no tears flowed on the airplane from Guangzhou China to Sydney Australia. My life was about to change, hopefully for the better but strangely I did not feel any emotion. Yes my life was changing but I would be resolute and do my best no matter what may happen.

Watching the pure white clouds floating in the dark blue sky, I let myself sink into my memories. Who was I at this moment? I am a 28 year old female, a typical product of Chinese single child policy, unmarried. This Chinese truth remained as China disappeared and within a single day, I walked inside an unknown future.

Almost every day I see the golden sunshine coloring Sydney city. The seven colors of the rainbow, like a silky belt connect the land and sky after a short summer shower. The sea water in Darling Harbor tastes yummy with a perfect proportion of salt. I got to taste the cold salty sea water during my first Jet Boating trip in Circular Quay. I felt so alive on that boat ride! The clean air excited me.

My study life in Sydney meant I could read a lot of interesting and relevant books related to my major, a Master of Management in the field of International Business. I was getting mature ideas and appreciating the different but outstanding personalities and characters of my tutors and classmates. Life was good. I found a share house at Croydon. I had my own room and was not far from the city so travel to university was really convenient. However, a few of life's events coloured the ideal world which formed my current reality.

### The Stubborn Girl and the Deceitful Restaurant Manager

As with all good life-planners, I started to look for a job in a restaurant to get some pocket money to make my study easier. I wrote some resumes and hand delivered them to places of interest. After two hours handing out my resumes, a Turkish restaurant showed some interest in me. The manager looked tidy in his crisp white shirt and black pants. I had a chance to have a trial that night as a kitchen hand and the offered salary was $14 per hour. Things looked good for a while but would not stay that way. The manager did not mention an unpaid trial time when he offered me $14 per hour.

After I had worked for three hours and a half, along with seven other hard working big men in that kitchen, washing dishes and chopping tomatoes, I found myself in the situation of an unpaid trial. I felt that I had been taken advantage of because of my trusting nature. The deception by the restaurant manager was the complete opposite of my personal values, so I rang the manager and argued with him, eventually threatening to call the police if I was not paid for what I was owed. The manager eventually relented and the tall, good looking chef was instructed to pay me $50, even though they considered me a bad tempered Chinese girl. Did I win that night? I don't know. Did I feel scared? I think yes. Anyway, I believe I have learnt to show my resolve in the face of unfairness and being taken advantage of. Sometimes, braveness works.

## The Asian Cultural Tradition Rams into Western Freedom

Nobody could bear the never-ending loneliness, except maybe God. No matter where we are, the desire for communication is natural and drives our behavior. Simply speaking, I needed to make friends. The important point was I need to figure out what kind of friends can be considered as true friends. Anyway, my thinking was much more oriental than I thought. As a 28 year old adult, I knew a way to make friends. The lavender colored dress, high heels and scarlet red lipstick made me popular with the bar crowd dancing to pop music under the shining Sagittarius star of the southern hemisphere. I successfully made friends, male and female, local young people similar to my age. I thought I was very lucky in this vast land until one day I attended a party with some of my friends. I felt my heart beginning to beat quicker than normal. The first reason was a feeling of excitement and eagerness to attend a local party, but then I saw some of my friends smoking water with black stuff inside. They had a special and kind of strange smile on their face. While I was still wondering and analyzing the situation, one of my friends asked me if I wanted to smoke that stuff. Naturally, I asked what it was and what they told me was a word that I had never heard before. I checked the meaning of the word on my mobile phone. When I realized what it was, I knew I was in a potentially dangerous situation. Since I was a child I was been educated to keep as far away as possible from dangerous situations and using drugs was a situation I was determined to avoid. I had been pure and honorable during my 28 years of life but I now found myself in a situation that people were undertaking an illegal activity and I felt very scared and isolated.

My Chinese education had tattooed the strict rules in my

mind and had no allowance to let that kind of over-freedom in. Suddenly I said I felt sick and dizzy. I immediately left the party and went outside. I finally began to calm down in the cool night air. Looking back at the time I was involved with my so called friends, the poker machines, drinks and rough times together, I didn't see anything positive. I came to realize that I had wasted a lot of my study time and also felt I had been contaminated. Obviously, if I allowed myself to be friends with these people, no doubt I would be one of them sooner or later.

This time, I felt that my cultural values saved me from dangerous western freedom. I deleted the relevant phone numbers and disappeared from my friends' sight.

### The Battle of the Final Exam

After the culture shock, I found out that I had two big issues. Firstly, my final exam was approaching in two weeks' time. Secondly, I became upset and started to worry and questioned the ethics of my behavior. I felt guilty about putting myself in a silly situation. However, I must finish my study and manage it well because this is the best chance I had after years of hard working in China. In my past life, I never allowed myself to run away from difficulties and now I will not change my hard attitude either.

Under the determination to pass the exams with the best results possible in such a short time, I borrowed books from the library and studied day and night. It seemed that only study could release the pressure inside me. I lost weight in this period but finally I got one pass and two credits in my three subjects. Of course, I will do better in the next semester.

Now my overseas study life continues as usual. After my first three months and feeling Australia in some deeper level, I have found my ability to hedge and manage risk is considerably enhanced. My ability to recognize and understand different people and situations has greatly improved; and suddenly my English level has improved as a result of my interaction with the local people.

## My First Warm Christmas and New Year Festival

Different to my known Santa Claus, who always prefers sitting in a sleigh and driven by the reindeers to deliver the gifts in cold Snowy night, the Australia Saint Clause likes to swim in the south Pacific sea or drinks some Pure Blonde (a Sydney local beer name) to keep cool in the hot summer. The 2013 New Year begins with my first over thirty degree January day. Jade green trees exercise themselves with the wind under dazzling sunshine. Time seems to stop in the night party in the local club just before 12 o'clock at New Year's Eve. People sing with joy and dance with excitement, giving best wishes to their loved ones and themselves on New Year's Eve.

Holding a glass of crystal white wine, I walked outside to the yard in the warm summer wind, allowing memories to flash back to when I was in Shanghai, China. It was such a cold and white 1st January from all the big snowing. I could only get warm through hot coffee and the reverse-cycle air conditioner. At that time there was no one beside me. Now in Australia, it is the same. I can't help myself to feel how life can be both changeable and remain the same simultaneously. Last year I cried in the cold winter for my loneliness, this year I smile to myself about the same thing in a different place. So I took out my phone to ring back to my own country in this warm night but couldn't stop the tears coming out when I heard the familiar and caring voice of my mother.

The process of transformation between two cultures is not an easy one and certainly not a straight path. It has brought pain and hurt, intertwined with mistakes and lessons. The best way to manage is to focus on the end goal, learn from mistakes and try new things but at the same time try my best to not lose my own values. I have overcome difficulties and became more tolerant and diversified in observing the world and different cultural values.

I now go to watch the beautiful view at Darling Harbor whenever I am free in the early evening. I have managed to focus on my study and firmly believe my life will be better tomorrow as the sun will rise again. A little bit of rain is also ok.

# St Madeleine's

## By Elaine Lavezzo

We met near St Mary's, the Notre Dame's styled gothic cathedral in heart of Sydney. Immediately I noticed her hair, the elegant bun she wore on the right side of the head instead of at the back. Madeleine was thin and tall, keeping her sophisticated way of walking, looking and observing things with her vivid blue eyes. She must be European, a French woman, I thought. Her delicate skin exquisitely wrinkled seemed to tell that she had travelled a lot around the world.

While serving the spicy smelled soup, I could bet that Madeleine's elegance came from Europe, by the way she said to the noisy friend sitting next to her:

– It is kind of a minestrone ...

Madeleine's delicate figure was illuminated by the full moon of a freezing Friday night. I wondered what sort of fairy tale had led her to that point of her life story which seemed to be more inspired in a Jean Genet play than in a Charles Perrault tale.

There was no pumpkin in the soup, just pieces of chicken, carrots, beans and spiced curry. There was no prince that fairy night, just pieces of human beings, hungry and homeless. Dozens of them, those warmly dressed homeless, like dwarfs of forgotten city streets. They had long, unkempt hair and open smiles, organized in long lines as if they believed that somewhere under the rainbow they could get some food over white plastic plates, I thought to myself.

One man had two damaged teddy bears over his chest, under his clothes. A grown up child with no memories of past, present or future. Suddenly he got on his knee as if he would pray for St Madeleine, and then screamed a few sentences in his own invented language, saying good night to the bears which lived inside his awakened dreams.

All of them, like the man, were from the kingdom of the homeless, and their blue-eyed poverty was simply looking for bread and soup to fill their bellies and some warmth on a cold night. Like refugees fleeing to the Charity of Oz.

When she finished her soup, Madeleine began to feed me with her true story.

– I was born in France, but then I went to Belgium during the 70s. Then I lived in Italy and Spain. I was married for forty years. Forty. But then my husband became violent, and began to beat me ...

Then her noisy friend interrupted the conversation, demanding Madeleine's attention:

– What do you think about this blazer on me?

– Oh, it fits you very properly, and it matches your green pants as well.

At that moment, she reminded me of Coco Chanel. Both of them were French, had a hard life and wore elegance in their bones. I wondered if Chanel could speak English as beautifully and politely ...

Then I asked Madeleine:

– Could you speak French to me?

– *Oui Madame, et je sais chanter aussi ... Quand il me prend dans ses bras, qu'il me parle tout bas, je vois la vie en rose, il me dit des mots damour des mots de tout les jours et ça me fait quelque chose ...*

All of a sudden the bell sounded nine times. DING-DONG-DING-DONG. And the blue eyes walked out into the night to their homes somewhere or nowhere. Like them, Madeleine disappeared in a flash, and she did not even leave one Cinderella shoe for me to catch.

The following Sunday at Mass in St Mary's Cathedral, I remembered Madeleine and I prayed for life to be kind to her and all those fantastic blue-eyed beings, their damaged teddy bears and their Friday night bread and soup. God bless the homeless of Commonwealth Australia!

# *Emily*

## By Emily Gu

In order to realize my dream of oversea study, I flew to Sydney from Guangzhou in the third day after I received my offer last year.

In my impression, westerners believe in God and always mention God when they talk. I can feel the existence of God and that god bless me after I got to Australia because I got a part-time job in a good company and the most important thing was that they pay me pretty good salary. I was moved. I haven't any local work experience and I just arrived in Sydney for no more than one month. But my boss is still willing to give me one chance.

Something really influences my mood so I cannot focus on my job and have made some mistakes at work. It caused complaint from my customer. My boss asked me not to go to work in the next two weeks. I felt that something bad might happen. So I go on internet and looked for another part-time job very anxiously.

One day after my previous job searching, I had got a chance of a trial job. I got on the train to go to one place located in western area for trial job. I am living in southern area. As the train going, I watched the scenery outside. The scenery of western area was different from that of southern area. I could not see many houses or building on the way. All that I can see is high grass and river. If southern area looks like small town, western area should be village, I thought.

My God! I needed to change train twice to get to the place where I have a trial job so I needed to spend a long time on the train. I took my iPhone from my bag to play with it to kill time. Actually I didn't enjoy playing with it. I was thinking that why I was so unlucky, my boss may never ask me to do that job just because I had made some mistakes. Why I saw the news from newspaper and got to know that some oversea students were able to earn enough living expense to support themselves.

It is no so easy. Not to mention local companies, even many Chinese companies were not willing to hire me because I was too fresh here. How can those oversea students do that? In fact, I know it is too difficult now. Even if I don't need to earn money to support my life and tuition fee in Sydney but I know I am not young, I don't want to depend on my parents any more. I want to reduce their economic burden.

I thought I could reply on my relatives before I came to Sydney but you will know that they are not willing to help me a lot at all. Because they have been fighting for their lives for so many years in foreign lands. Now they have everything so why should they help you to gain what they have now so quickly. You should fight for everything by yourself, just like what they did at the beginning. Now I know that relatives actually will not treat you good even if they know that your life is difficult here. Sometimes even a stranger here will give me a help without requiring a return. These several days, I was full of negative energy. All in my mind was unhappy matters happened these days.

On the train, I noticed that a man was sitting opposite to me, but I didn't care him too much because I was focusing on my iPhone. Suddenly a red rose appear in front of me:

"Merry Christmas!" A gentle voice came to my ears. I almost forget that Christmas was coming because I was too busy with my studying and looking for a part time job. He held a red rose and handed it to me. It was just a rose not a bunch of roses but it suddenly drew me out of depression.

"Thank you!" I smiled finally.

"How do you celebrate your Christmas?"

"I don't know! Maybe I will not celebrate my Christmas because I need to work at that time. Also, I have no friends here so no one will celebrate with me."

"I am sorry to hear that! You have to work?"

"Yes."

"You need money."

"Yes, because I want to depend on myself!"

The man was around thirty to forty years old, not well dressed, took a canvas bag stuffed with something and a bunch of flowers. The bag and wrapper of flowers looked very simple, just like his dressing. The man came to sit with me and began to search something from his bag. I was wondering that whether he was searching some money for me. Yes, he did! He took out a twenty dollar note to me. I felt very shocked. This kind of matter never happened on me even if I had been living on the world for nearly thirty years.

"Take it! You can take it to buy some gadgets or snacks you want."

I felt a little bit embarrassed because I was afraid that it would let him think that I was greedy but I never spent money on buying things which I didn't need except necessary supplies. The twenty dollar was so attractive to me. I said no and thank you. But he insisted on giving it on me.

In my impression, there are many churches in Sydney. There must be at least one in each suburb. People believe god here. They will say god bless you if they want to express their appreciation for you, I really feel that god exist here because every time when I feel depressed, someone who are strangers will do something to make you feel better. It seems that god let me know that he will not leave me alone when I feel sad or depressed. What happened today is just one of the examples.

I didn't know what to say just said thank you. But I felt so warm in my heart. It just like someone sent you the fire in a cold snowy winter. That man said goodbye and took off the train. I felt that I had got power suddenly. After second change at the train station, I finally arrived at the place where I had a trial job. Streets were narrower than where I was living; it was about one time narrower than my streets. Tone of the advertisement in the street or decoration of shops tended to be darker, not as bright as the southern area. Anyway, it was another round of scenery.

I searched the GPS from my iPhone and tried to find the exact location of the place where I had a trial job. Walking along the street, I found a club in the front of me. Finally I found it. It was a club seemed like RSL but their businesses were not very busy. The club was spacious and there were bars, restaurants and game machines there. You could have different choices for your meals. It was really a good place to have an entertainment when you were free or after job. The place where I had a trial job was a western restaurant but the boss is a Chinese. I gave him a call and he asked me to go into the kitchen. The kitchen was the place where I mainly stay to do the job. There were one girl and one chef in the kitchen. It was a small business. The man was the boss of the restaurant and the only one chef as well. He had only one employee. I was wondering why bosses of Chinese restaurant in Australia would do the job of chef because in my mind bosses would never do the job in person in China. They are just responsible for purchasing the food, arranging the duties and monitoring workers. But here bosses will all do the job of chefs as well. Maybe because the labor is quite expensive here so bosses could not afford it. They will earn very little money if they hire a chef.

The kitchen was not large but not so crowded as the one of china town. I remembered that in china town, the kitchen was much smaller than this one but it accommodated three to four people. In addition, the air was full of oil and there was plenty of dirty water on the floor. It would be easy for you to fall down. However, it was respectively cleaner and tidier here and the working atmosphere was very leisure. The boss asked the girl to teach me how to do the job.

First of all, I should try to remember the menu, figure out where to put different kitchen ware and learn how to wash the dishes. Thanks goodness! I hated washing dishes. I just need to use water to flush off dishes simply and then put them into a washing machine. I thought it was a position of waitress but actually it was a restaurant all rounder. Also, I needed to do some simple cooking if the boss were too busy such as putting meat into oil to deep fry or roasting the bread. The oven and oil were very hot so I was a little bit scared of them. For a woman who doesn't do housework very often, just like me, it is a little hard to handle these things. The worst thing was that the boss asked me to take the sizzling steak out of the kitchen to customers. I should not only take one dish out of the kitchen to customer in one of my hand, but also take another dish in my other hand. I needed to take dishes in both of my hands to customers. I tried to hold the sizzling steak in my hand but I could not do it because I was scared that the hot oil will hurt my hand.

"Ah ... it is hot!" I tried to take the sizzling steak in my hand.

"You take it to the customers. Don't let her to do it. It is not good if she falls down," the boss said to the girl.

The girl took two dishes in both of her hands very easily and took them to customers. How can she do it? Isn't she afraid that the hot oil will hurt her hands? It was such a trifle but I still could not handle it. When I was thinking how to handle this matter well if I got the job, the boss had finished the dinner for me and the girl and asked me to have it. There were noodles and fish in a bowl of soup. It was not very delicious food but better than no dinner.

The girl was studying in high school and very nice. We had dinner together and chatted with each other just like friends. After finished dinner, she continued to teach me how to do the job. Then she asked me to try to use water to flush off dishes. The tap was connected with a very long stainless steel tube and set at a high holder. Once I pressed the button, strong water would come out. I think all restaurant kitchen will use this kind of tap. It was easy to wash away the residue of food because the water was strong enough. The basin was very deep and might be 80 centimeter in depth. What I need to do was to control the strength of water and figure out the correct posture. The girl showed me how to do it and it seemed quite simple for her. But it was not easy for me to do it correctly when I tried it. The girl seemed a little impatient maybe I was too stupid. However, I washed twenty or thirty dishes totally.

After two hours trial job, the boss asked me to stop and told me the trial job had finished. I could go home now. I knew that it was not a good news because boss would do so if he was not satisfied with your performance. Although I didn't have too much local work experience but it was common sense to know that probably the boss would not hire me. But I still kept a good attitude and said good bye to him. The girl seemed to know the fact too and showed a little sympathy with me. Until that moment, I knew she was a girl with a good heart.

I was not very upset maybe I had good experience on the train before the trial job. Anyway, I know maybe I really don't suitable for catering industry. I had tried several trial jobs for the position of waitress before but finally the boss didn't decide to hire me. I knew that doing housework was very important at that moment. Maybe I would get the job if I did housework at home rather than leaving all them to my mum. Anyway I just realize that I didn't suitable for a job but I had done nothing hurt to anybody. I was still a good lady and I failed an unsuitable job. It was not a big deal at all.

At that moment, I knew that I shouldn't feel so blue as before because there still be some wonderful things happening to me. I shouldn't be so negative and tried to focus on wonderful things but not only jobs. Just like a song I heard before, life doesn't always go your way. I shouldn't feel frustrated so quickly. Just insisting on what I need to do every day and never give up, I believed that good luck will happen on me one day.

"The next station will be Glenfield!" the broadcaster said.

It stopped my thinking. Suddenly I realized I should get off the train and change to another line.

# The Authors

## Lili Wu

Lili Wu, Chinese, holds a Master of Management (International Business), a Bachelor of English and American Literature, and is currently studying Master of Professional Accounting at Central Queensland University.

Lili has been an English teacher, fabric merchandiser, waitress, student, an optimist in life, and a long time volunteer to an Australian national charity, The Smith Family.

### Elaine Lavezzo

Elaine Lavezzo is a Brazilian educator and journalist, who is very involved with community activities concerning culture, environment and education. Due to her engagement with community projects, Ms Lavezzo had the honor of being the only Brazilian to be granted an Australian Awards Scholarship. The AusAID scholarship provided her the opportunity of doing a Master of Professional Education at Central Queensland University.

During her stay in Australia, Elaine volunteered with Australian NGOs Mission Australia and Exodus Foundation helping homeless, immigrant and refugee communities. She was also involved with the Tree of Life drama group, which performs a play about the journey of refugee children.

While completing her scholarship, Elaine took part in a

"Writing Memoir" course with the Australian writer Claire Scobie and, then, did "Writing a play" course at the NSW Writers´ Centre. During the course, Ms Lavezzo wrote the play "Refugees" mentored by the Australian playwright Timothy Daly, who is now her PhD supervisor at the University of Wollongong.

### Emily Gu

Emily is an international student studying a Master's degree of Professional Accounting in Central Queensland University, Sydney campus. She has been working in China for four years and quit her last job in a Singapore bank for further study in Australia. She came to Australia alone and has experienced sweetness and bitterness in her journey. However, she appreciates God's support and help and is determined to try her best to finish her study in Australia.

## The Editors

### Professor Donna Lee Brien

Donna Lee Brien is Professor, Creative Industries, at Central
Queensland University. She has taught creative and professional
writing for the past two decades. Extensively published, Donna's
biography *John Power 1881-1943* is the standard work on this expa-
triate artist, and she is author of over twenty exhibition catalogues
and other books including the bestselling trade self-help *Girls*

*Guide* series (with Tess Brady). Donna is Commissioning Editor, Special Issues, *TEXT: Journal of Writing and Writing Courses*, and Past President, Australasian Association of Writing Programs. Donna's most recent book, reflecting her interest in writing about death, edited with Lorna Piatti-Farnell, is *New Directions in 21st Century Gothic: The Gothic Compass*, Routledge, New York and London, 2015.

## Associate Professor Alison Owens

Alison Owens is an adjunct Associate Professor of Education at Central Queensland University. She has taught university courses in English, education, communications, literacy and social research methods for over twenty years and has a special interest in internationalization of education and curriculum as well as second language learning. She has researched and published widely in academic journals on these topics and has been the recipient of multiple research grants. Alison is the current recipient of an Australian government scholarship to undertake a PhD in creative writing at CQUniversity. She has had short stories published in Australian magazines and is currently working on an historical fiction set in Sydney in the mid 20th century.

## Dr Janene Carey

Janene Carey is a freelance writer, editor and academic. She has a PhD in writing, and her work has been published in national newspapers, magazines and literary journals, including the *Sydney Morning Herald*, the *Sun-Herald*, OUTBACK magazine, *Great Australians*, *Australian Book Review*, TEXT and *Perilous Adventures*. She is the author of a narrative nonfiction book called *A Hospital Bed at Home: Family stories of caregiving from diagnosis to death*. Her website is www.janenecarey.com

www.ingramcontent.com/pod-product-compliance
Lightning Source LLC
Chambersburg PA
CBHW020444030426
42337CB00014B/1392